GOD
THE INGENIOUS
ALCHEMIST

GOD
THE INGENIOUS
ALCHEMIST

Transforming Tragedy into Blessing

JOHN R. CLAYPOOL

Church Publishing
NEW YORK

Copyright © 2005 by John R. Claypool

Church Publishing
19 East 34th Street
New York, NY 10016
www.churchpublishing.org

Cover art: "Joseph Greeting Jacob in Egypt" (Anonymous, nineteenth century lithograph) courtesy of Image Select / Art Resource, NY.

Cover design: Corey Kent

Library of Congress Cataloging-in-Publication Data

Claypool, John.
    God, the ingenious alchemist : transforming tragedy into blessing / John R. Claypool.
        p. cm.
ISBN 0-8192-2180-5 (hardcover)
ISBN 978-1-64065-086-2 (pbk.)
1. Bible. O.T. Genesis—Criticism, interpretation, etc. I. Title.
    BS1235.52C53 2005
    248.8'6—dc22
                                2004024056

Printed in the United States of America

TO ALL THOSE
through whom The Ingenious Alchemist is working
to promote my healing from cancer,
especially Doctors Melvin Moore and Omar Najjar,
the wonderful people on their staffs,
all the incredible folks who work in
The Kann Center of DeKalb General Hospital,
the many dear ones who pray for and encourage me,
and my devoted caregiver who never leaves my side,
my beloved wife, Ann

Contents

Acknowledgments

The love of stories was instilled in me as a very young child. I was born into a large Southern family that filled every reunion with marvelous tales and narratives, and I spent untold hours as a child sitting in church hearing Baptist preachers tell illustration after illustration that were largely narrative in character. All of these influences created in me a lifelong affection for the story form of truth, a predilection that drew me to that great collection of narratives that are found in the book of Genesis.

In the early 1960s, a controversy over this part of Holy Scripture erupted in the denomination to which I then belonged, the Southern Baptist Convention, and I responded to this crisis by preaching a series of sermons on the first eleven chapters of Genesis. This was my first serious homiletical venture on the very first book of the Old Testament, and it deepened my appreciation of this particular book and initiated what would be the first of many teaching and preaching projects for me over the next four and a half decades.

Across the years I have conducted a large number of short-term and even year-long studies of the book of Genesis, and have been shaped and reshaped repeatedly by the dialogue that these presentations evoked between those who listened and responded, especially at the last two parishes that I served full time—Christ Episcopal Church in San Antonio, Texas, and Saint Luke's Episcopal Church in Birmingham, Alabama. My most recent experience with the book of Genesis came in the fall of 2001, when I began teaching homiletics at the McAfee School of Theology in Atlanta, Georgia, and I used the whole book of Genesis as the basis for courses during two semesters. What is contained in this short volume is the distillation of some forty-five years of "asking, seeking, and knocking" regarding the truths of this ancient and inspired segment of Holy Scripture.

The actual formulation of this book was a genuine collaboration with my beloved wife and best friend, Ann. She not only typed and retyped the many drafts that make up the creation of any manuscript, but she also thoughtfully and carefully helped me restate and clarify sentence after sentence of the whole project. It would not be an overstatement to describe her as a "co-author" of this book, for without her this work would be entirely different and inferior to its present form. Her interest and encouragement, not only in this book, but also in the whole of my life, are clearly the greatest graces I have ever known, and all that she is and has done for me are beyond my powers of expression.

I must also acknowledge the creative part that Debra Farrington of Morehouse Publishing has played in this endeavor. We first met at a conference at the Kanuga Episcopal Retreat Center in North Carolina in 2002, and our friendship has also been a great blessing in my life. She and her colleagues at Morehouse have greatly improved the quality of this book by their thorough editorial efforts, and my gratitude for their contributions is great indeed.

Only the Holy One is truly original—the rest of us are simply passing on to others what we have first received. I am the beneficiary of countless numbers of authors, interpreters, articulate friends, and even critics. My highest hope is that I can do for others in these pages what has been done *so* graciously for me.

John R. Claypool
Atlanta, Georgia

Introduction

Over three decades ago, I heard a well-known Presbyterian minister, Dr. Ernest Campbell, make an observation that impressed me very deeply. He said, "There are two great moments in every human being's life—the moment when one is born and the moment when one begins to discover why he or she was born." I sense great truth in that affirmation. It not only points to that moment of sheer grace, when we come out of nothing into being because of a generous act of God, but also to the mystery and wonder of genuine spiritual experience, when the reality of the Holy ceases to be merely a mental concept and becomes an authentic event. In my own case, there was an eighteen-year differential between these two, which is probably not that unusual given what William James referred to as "the variety of religious experience." No two human beings are exactly alike, which means that the shape of all of our encounters will always be characterized by profound uniqueness.

I would like to add that a similar parallel exists between the realm of the personal and the theological. My point here is that there are also two great moments when it comes to our relationship to that Ultimate Mystery who lies behind all things: namely, the moment when one senses the existence of such a Reality and then the moment when one begins to image more clearly and insightfully what that One is truly like. In my own experience, the first of these moments was a telling event that took place unexpectedly in my room in a college dormitory. Suddenly and quite surprisingly, I felt myself encompassed and surrounded by Something utterly other than my own being and, with that sense of accompaniment, came an affirmation somewhat similar to Moses' encounter at the burning bush on Mount Sinai when he heard the words, "I am the Lord your God." Part of the amazing impact of this experience was a sense that the Holy One was saying to me, "I do in fact exist!" That epiphany was the beginning of the adult phase of my spiritual pilgrimage and a decisive turning point for me religiously. It set the stage for the second part of my theological quest, which was to discern more precisely what this One, whom I had come to believe actually existed, was really like. This spiritual pilgrimage involved an imaging process that has continued to unfold for over fifty years now and is still very open and dynamic. As St. Paul asserts, we humans will always "know in part and prophesy in part," when it comes to our perceptions. We do indeed "see as through a glass darkly," particularly with regard to understanding the Holy One, which means that we should never be dogmatic or arrogant about our theological insights. Realizing that there is more in God than we can ever fully know, we can sense certain aspects of the Mystery and share our witness with each other as honest gifts, rather than sledgehammer absolutes imposed coercively on others.

My purpose in this volume is to share with you something of my own discoveries in this quest to know more of what God is really like. Please regard what you will encounter in the following pages as "the first words of an ongoing conversation," not "the last word" on anything that precludes further exploration and discussion. Also, I want to acknowledge that the very first book in the Bible, called Genesis, will be the primary resource from which I will draw my insights. I will refer initially to an image that grows out of the first two chapters of that remarkable document, but the bulk of the material comes from the last half of Genesis, specifically chapters twenty-five through fifty. These intriguing stories revolve around a man named Jacob and the twelve sons who made up such an important part of his life.

The image of the Holy One that has emerged for me from these stories is the title of this book: *God, The Ingenious Alchemist.* Let me describe what I mean by these words and then use those wonderful old narratives to illustrate and, hopefully, illumine for you this particular insight into the nature of the Holy One.

My beginning point is the answer that the first two chapters of Genesis give to the question that theologian Paul Tillich claimed launched him on his life-long theological quest. As an adolescent, he found himself pondering that most primordial question, "Why something and not nothing?" Why did anything come to *exist,* a word that means literally "standing out of nothingness"? The accounts of creation in Genesis chapters one and two give me the sense that in the time before time, in the world beyond our world, something truly significant must have taken place. The Ultimate Mystery behind all things—the One who is life, has life, and possesses the power to give life—the One who across the ages has been called God—must have said, "This wonder of my existence is something too good to keep to myself. I want others to experience the ecstasy of aliveness and to share the essence of the joy that is the very heart of my Being."

As a result of that impulse, the Holy One began to create, not to get something for God's Self, but rather to give something of God's Self. What I am affirming is that generosity was the primal motivation that caused all things to come out of nothingness into existence. It was an act of total and complete graciousness. Medieval theologians used to speak of "the unnecessary-ness of creation." There is no hint in either creation account of there being any lack in God or any selfish motive that prompted this One to act. The process of giving life to "all things visible and invisible" was, in C. S. Lewis's words, an act of unabashed "gift-love." According to Genesis, such generosity of spirit is our reason for being, the ultimate reason to explain "why something and not nothing."

If you allow such a perspective to serve as your beginning assumption, it leads to a further question: what qualities would creatures need to possess in order to experience God's unique form of ecstasy? Would it not follow that, in addition to existence itself, creatures capable of this kind of joy would need the capacities of personhood, which include a certain amount of power to make things happen and a measure of genuine freedom? In the absence of these qualities, God's kind of joy would be impossible. It is very hard to imagine a rock or a turtle having several options from which to choose, acting decisively and then exclaiming, "It is good! It is good! It is very, very good!" This is how Genesis images the Holy One, and participating in this One's kind of delight necessitates being made in the image of all these qualities. Not even an utterly omnipotent God could make God's kind of joy accessible to others without granting both real potency and genuine freedom to them.

I agree with Simone Weil, who once observed, "Creation is the moment when God ceased to be everything so that humans could be something." Had not the Creator genuinely shared some of the Creator's power and passed it into hands of real freedom, the goal that motivated the whole enterprise would have been unachievable. Those qualities that lie at the heart of all personal realities are essential ingredients of the fulfilling of God's desire for others to know God's kind of ecstasy.

Sober recognition of these assertions will quickly make it obvious that an enormous risk was inherent in this grand adventure of God's generosity. If freedom is truly free, there is no anticipating how it will be exercised in the future. The same ancient document that affirms God's reason for creating also records that, for reasons that are never fully clear, the humans who were called into being in order to experience God's joy, abused their freedom and moved in the opposite direction! The reality of evil is totally irrational. Why would entities that are capable of joy choose misery and destructiveness instead? It makes no sense at all. Psychologist and popular writer Scott Peck's little boy once observed that the word *evil* is the word *live* spelled backwards. Hold a mirror up to the letters *l-i-v-e* and you see the word *evil,* which is what the Bible calls "the mystery of iniquity." It is an ultimate absurdity but, tragically, this is the response that the earliest humans made to God's primal generosity. They proceeded to unmake creation. God started with nothing and moved through chaos to form and beauty, but ungrateful creatures reversed that process and turned form and beauty back into chaos, toward the nothingness from which all came. This process involves "the death-wish" that Sigmund Freud found so deeply imbedded in the human psyche. Evil goes against all that is vital, creative, and meaningful, and yet it became a part of human history and remains a potent force up to this very moment.

According to Genesis, this dark turn of what began as a joyful adventure brought utter anguish to the heart of God. This dismantling of creation and the introduction of pain and chaos into human experience were not what the Joyful One had intended at all. The book of Genesis makes it clear, in the story of Noah and the flood (Genesis 7–9), that God seriously considered giving up on creation altogether and allowing humanity to return to the nothingness from which it came. However, at the last minute, so to speak, something even more momentous than the Holy One becoming the Generous One is recorded as having occurred. In a mystery even greater than "the mystery of iniquity," the Generous One chose to become the Merciful One and, instead of abandoning rebellious humanity, God chose the path of redemption and restoration. The Holy One set out on a process even more amazing than the generosity of creation. God resolved to do all that unconditional love could do to correct what C. S. Lewis called the "bentness of spirit" that is the source of evil. The amazing grace that lies at the heart of salvation history is the theme of the whole biblical story.

Where did the Holy One find the courage to embark on such a daunting response? Here is what led me to the image that is the central focus of this book. My contention is that behind the wonder that prompted the Generous One to become the Merciful One was not only unconditional love and compassion, but also trust in God's ingenious ability to take bad choices made in human freedom and somehow transmute them into experiences of growth and blessing. I find the image of an "alchemist" quite helpful here. Alchemists were those ancient pioneers in the realm of science who kept trying to find a way to transform lead into gold. They wanted to take one kind of substance and make it into something else. I believe that, in addition to generosity and unconditional love, God possesses the gift that eluded the ancient alchemists. This One who, according to St. Paul, "gives life to the dead and calls into existence the things that do not exist" (Romans 4:17) is alone in all the world in having this kind of ingenuity. Without robbing human beings of the freedom that is utterly essential to their reason for being, God has within God's being the ability to take bad things or events and resourcefully bring good out of them.

I propose a diagram to illustrate this daring theological claim. Imagine two concentric circles in which the inner circle represents genuine human freedom and the outer circle represents Divine Ingenuity, which permeates the entire universe. In other words, regardless of how an individual chooses to come out of his or her circle of freedom, that action enters the surrounding realm of God's Divine Ingenuity in which the possibilities of redemption, growth, and blessing are always present.

To use another metaphor that points in the same direction, imagine a celestial card game. In the beginning, God holds the whole deck of cards, but the desire to share God's joy prompts God to deal some of God's power to the human beings around the table. This means that such empowered creatures have the capacity to play the hands that they have been dealt as they wish or to act in any way that they choose, for their freedom is authentic. However, the essence of the biblical story is that, while sharing God's power with others, God remains at the table and in the game as the Ingenious Alchemist!

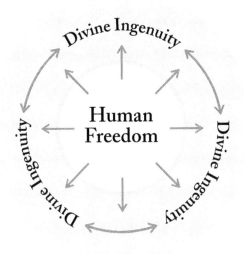

This is the image of the Divine that I now want you to witness at work in the stories of Jacob and his family. I will point to countless examples in which egregiously wrong human actions are redemptively transformed into occasions of growth and blessing. The purpose of all this is to open for you a pathway to hope and to make it possible for you to believe that, through thick and thin and the very worst of times, the Ingenious Alchemist can still do the best of things. It is this theological vision that can enable you to move from a life of fear and despair to a life of courage and hopeful coping.

GOD

THE INGENIOUS
ALCHEMIST

CHAPTER 1

God Lives at the End of Our Ropes

The Early Life of Jacob: Genesis 25–28

It has long been a conviction of mine that the document we call the Holy Bible is deeply and profoundly true, with the added proviso that contained within its covers are many distinct forms of truth. The Good Book, as it is often described, is a many-splendored thing, a variety of forms of truth as to how God has revealed God's self, including historical facts, haunting and lovely poetry, pithy proverbs, lengthy genealogies, parabolic stories, and wildly imaginative apocalyptic scenarios, to name only a few. All of these varied forms qualify for the adjective *true*, and one of the most powerful of these forms is biographical narrative. What I propose to do is take some of the stories in the last half of the book of Genesis that revolve around a man named Jacob and his sons, and use them to illustrate the image of God as the Ingenious Alchemist. As I have already stated in the Introduction, I think one of the most telling insights into the nature of the Holy One in all of Scripture is that of One who possesses the amazing ability to take the most destructive things of which we free creatures are capable and transmute them into occasions of positive growth and blessing. What the ancient alchemists tried to do in turning the substance of lead into gold is a vivid image of this most incredible divine characteristic.

The author Frederick Buechner had little formal religious exposure or training until he became a well-educated young adult. In his late twenties, when he first began to encounter seriously the words of Holy Scripture, he reports that his greatest surprise was how, again and again, "the seemingly worst things were never the last things." He discovered that the God of Holy Scripture always seemed to have something up God's amazing sleeve, and I offer this image as a seminal insight into the very heart of that Mystery who stands behind all reality. In trying to understand why certain things happen, like the tragedies of 9/11/01, or where God was in the midst of such anguished events, I believe that this particular image can shed real light and become a means of deepening a sense of faith rather than destroying it. The early life of the patriarch Jacob is illustrative of this particular insight.

Jacob was the grandson of Abraham, who was the legendary "father of faith" and the true fountainhead of the Hebrew nation. Abraham was the one to whom God had appeared and promised to bless the whole human family through his descendants. Jacob and his twin brother, Esau, were Abraham's grandsons through his son, Isaac. While Isaac's wife, Rebecca, had been carrying these two, she experienced great internal struggle and was informed by an oracle that the twins and their descendants would engage in awesome conflict and the younger son would come to have preeminence over the older brother. At the moment of delivery, Esau emerged first from Rebecca's womb, which meant that he was technically regarded as the firstborn and eldest son and, in that era, this was an issue of huge importance. The technical term for this tradition is "primogeniture," in which all manner of privilege was accorded to the oldest male child. The eldest son inherited a lion's share of the father's property and was given the responsibility of being the leader of the family in every way. However, as these two individuals grew and matured, it became increasingly obvious that they were radically different in both native gifts and temperaments.

Esau was an outdoorsman through and through, a hunter and a fisherman who was totally engrossed in the physical dimensions of life and had little interest in anything intellectual or spiritual. Jacob, on the other hand, was the polar opposite. He cherished matters of the mind and heart and was particularly sensitive to the fact that his grandfather Abraham had been entrusted with a religious vocation that had to be handed on intentionally from one generation to another. One of the differences between natural religion and a historical faith is located at this very point. It has often been observed that, given the shape of the biblical faith, "God has no grandchildren." The truth is that both the Hebrew and Christian religions are always within one generation of extinction. If believers in either one of these groups fail to pass on the stories of what God has done and is doing in history, these particular religious traditions will fade from the earth. There has to be an ongoing process of witnessing and, as Isaac's two sons grew into manhood, it became obvious both to Rebecca and Jacob that Esau would never go to the trouble of passing on the truths about "the God of Abraham and Isaac." Here is where the old tradition of primogeniture would have been lethal to the survival of the Abrahamic faith, so Rebecca and Jacob dared to do something considered most radical in the era in which they lived. Out of their desire to save something they treasured, they challenged the accepted notion of the primacy of the firstborn by committing two highly manipulative and deceptive acts.

There were two symbols of primogeniture in that time: a birthright and a patriarchal blessing passed on in the father's waning days. Jacob easily found a way to snare the transfer of the birthright from Esau. The ancient "good ol' boy" came in from hunting one afternoon and, in a famished panic, asked his younger brother to fix him some food. Jacob shrewdly proposed to do so if Esau would cede his firstborn right in exchange. True to his personal hierarchy of values, Esau reasoned, "Of what use is something as intangible as that, if one is starving to death? Of course, you can have the birthright," and without delay Jacob provided "a mess of pottage," thereby occasioning a crucial spiritual reality to change hands.

Some time later, Isaac realized his days were numbered and asked Esau to go hunt for wild game, then return, and, over a sacred meal, Isaac planned to confer on Esau the powerful patriarchal blessing. Rebecca overheard this exchange and quickly saw an opportunity to secure this treasure for Jacob rather than Esau. She cleverly orchestrated a process of deception by which blind and feeble old Isaac was shamelessly deceived. Rebecca dressed Jacob in animal skin to resemble the hairy older son, and she prepared the kind of meal Esau would have put together. Thus, Rebecca and Jacob were able to effect this exploitation of both Isaac and Esau. While faintly suspicious that something was wrong, the pathetic old blind man placed his hands on Jacob's head and said the sacred words of blessing. When Esau arrived later and the father and son realized what had taken place, Isaac was devastated and Esau was filled with fury at this utterly devious power play.

I want to pause for a moment and recall how, as a child, I used to puzzle over this particular story. I wondered, "Why did not Isaac take back the blessing that he had said over Jacob, once the deception was discovered, and then proceed to give Esau what was technically his by right?" What I later learned was that the ancient Hebrews had a high regard for the potency of the spoken word. They regarded the sounds that proceeded from a person's mouth to be exactly like arrows shot from a bow or rocks propelled from a sling. In their thinking, words were deeds and, once something was said, it assumed a life of its own and moved into the situation in which it was spoken with a power of its own. The important thing was that once a word was pronounced, it could not be retrieved. Isaac was incapable of recalling that spoken blessing once it had been said. There is a profound truth, of course, to this concrete understanding of human speech. Centuries later someone composed the following poem:

Boys flying kites, pull in their white-winged birds,
But this you cannot do, when you are flying words.
Thoughts, unexpressed, may some day fall back dead,
But God himself can't kill them, once they're said!
(Author unknown)

I find this to be a very sobering realization. I imagine that most of you can relate to the destructive power of words spoken, for example, in cruel gossip aimed at damaging or obliterating another's reputation.

Esau knew that his opportunity for the blessing had been missed once and for all, and he angrily resolved to kill

Jacob with his own bare hands as soon as their violated old father died. Rebecca heard of his intentions and knew that they were not an idle threat. There were many things this outdoorsman could not do, but as a hunter, he was more than capable of putting these words into action. Shrewd and resourceful as always, Rebecca took Jacob aside and told him that he had no choice but to flee for his life. Rebecca and Jacob had violated one of the most revered traditions of their society and radicals of every era have experienced the explosive reactions that always come from doing things differently from "the way we've always done things." Rebecca told Jacob that her brother, Laban, lived hundreds of miles to the east of Palestine in the section of Mesopotamia from which all the Abrahamic clan had migrated decades before. She said emphatically, "You must go there right away. Laban will give you sanctuary once you identify yourself as my son. There is no time to waste. Be gone this very hour!"

Such a proposal made all kinds of practical sense, but Jacob was initially overwhelmed by such a prospect. Remember, Esau was the outdoorsman and the hunter and Jacob was a gentle homebody. He had lived close to his mother, largely within the tents of the clan. He was the intellectual and the mystic of the family, and had never so much as spent a night very far from the protective company of his kindred. He did not have the first clue how to survive in the wild and, to make matters worse, people in that day and age traveled in groups, never alone. Only criminal outcasts ever ventured out by themselves, and there were few markers in those ancient times that pointed to the far-off land of Mesopotamia. Therefore, as realistic as Rebecca's proposal sounded, it must have evoked unmitigated terror throughout Jacob's whole being. Nevertheless, he was wily enough to realize that "some odds are better than no odds at all." In fear and trembling, he gathered together what few things he could manage to carry and made a hasty escape before the characteristically obtuse Esau realized what had happened.

No change of circumstances could have been more absolute or drastic for Jacob. He had awakened that morning in the same context in which he had lived all his life but, before the sun went down that same day, he found himself all alone on an unfamiliar rocky hilltop outside the ancient city of Luz. Jacob was in desperate straits indeed, feeling as though the bottom had fallen out of his life. One does not need a lot of imagination to contemplate what must have been flooding through the consciousness of this frightened fugitive. I am sure he was filled with all kinds of terror. He may have wondered, "Will some wild animal sniff me out in the night, pounce on me, and devour me? Will someone see me alone, assume I am a dangerous criminal, and kill me in what they think is self-defense? How on earth am I going to find my way to Uncle Laban and, even if I get to him, will he believe who I am and offer me hospitality?"

We all know that one of the ways we can severely traumatize ourselves is to play the game "What if?" Who would not be unsettled in thinking, "What if I have a heart attack or develop cancer? What if my spouse dies or the stock market crashes?" We can drive ourselves to the brink of despair by imagining the terrible things that might happen to us, and Jacob was probably overwhelmed by all kinds of fears.

At the same time, he may have also found himself seething with anger at the whole tradition of the firstborn being the recipient of most of the power and privileges. He may have raged against the idea that native gifts did not count for anything. He could have been angry with his mother also, for having treasured the old stories about

Abraham. Remember, Isaac had been through a frightening experience when he was twelve years old and his father had taken him up on a mountain and almost killed him before an angel stopped Abraham. One can understand how, after that trauma, Isaac never had much interest in the realm of religion. He made it a point to keep a discreet distance from this mysterious Being called God. The Scripture reports that he only prayed one time in his life. Thus, Isaac attached little value to the tradition of his father. It was Rebecca who deemed all this as important, and Jacob could easily have resented her for this and the crisis that resulted from it. What is obvious is that Jacob was traumatized by what he feared and felt at that moment on the hilltop outside of Luz.

I have to believe that he had enough sense of fairness in the depths of his being that he was experiencing guilt as well, for what he had done to both Esau and his father. While by no means the only truth, the famous Golden Rule does represent a basic form of relational maturity. As we measure how we would like other people to treat us, we get a clear sense of how we ought to treat other people. Lying there in the dark, I imagine Jacob had to come to terms with the fact that if Esau had done to him what he had done to Esau, he would have been enraged. Likewise, if any of his sons were to deceive him when he became old and weak, in the way that he had deceived his father, he would be just as infuriated. Let's face it; even a thief thinks stealing is wrong when he is being robbed!

It is hard to imagine a tougher situation than the one in which Jacob found himself at this particular moment. He was probably ashamed and regretful about the past, uneasy about the present, and fearful and apprehensive about the future. Yet, somehow, with nothing but a rock for his pillow, he managed finally to go to sleep, only to have something absolutely incredible happen. Jacob had a great dream in which he saw a ladder rooted in heaven above descending down to that lonely spot where he laid. Angels were moving up and down this ladder, and the Lord God himself appeared at the top of the ladder and said, "I am the God of Abraham and of Isaac." At that point, the Holy One called Jacob by name and said, "The land where you are sleeping is someday going to be given to your descendants. I am going to protect you on this journey you are taking today and I will eventually bring you back." In other words, Jacob was told that God was going to be with him and for him, in spite of everything he had done. Here is a genuine miracle. In a place where he least expected it and at a time when he least deserved it, grace happened to Jacob in a most amazing way.

A lady I once knew by the name of Gert Behanna had grown up with a father who was absolutely hostile toward all religion. He was very successful and had made a lot of money, but he refused to have anything to do with the spiritual realm of existence. As a result, Gert had no religious training whatsoever while she was a growing up, and she was given no moral compass by which to guide her behavior. Her adult experiences went from bad to worse. She married three times, only to have each marriage end up in divorce. She had two sons, whom she had no idea how to handle, and who wound up causing her all sorts of problems. In the midst of all this, she became increasingly dependent upon alcohol until, finally, her life became so unworkable that she said, "I cannot stand it any longer!" One night she took a massive overdose of sleeping pills, as a way to end her terrible agony and escape into what she thought would be final oblivion.

Imagine her dismay when, eight hours later, she woke up in the Intensive Care Unit of a hospital and had to face the fact that that she was such an inept failure that she could not even succeed in ending her life. Her despair became greater than ever. Not long after this rude awakening, some friends came to visit her and, in the simplest of ways, one of them said, "Gert, have you ever considered asking God into your life to help you with all that you are up against?" Gert replied angrily, "I don't even believe that there is a God! I am sick unto death of all this religious talk. It is just a crutch. You make God sound like some kind of bellhop who will come and carry your bags for you." Her friend replied nondefensively, "You know, a crutch is a wonderful help when you are crippled, and so is a bellhop when you have more baggage than you can carry."

The conversation ended there and her friends eventually went on their way. However, as Gert was lying there alone in the darkness, she looked up at the ceiling and stammered out, "God, I don't even know whether you exist. I have never had anything to do with you, but if you do exist and if you can help me, please, please come. I am absolutely at the end of my rope."

Lo and behold, just like the experience of Jacob, at a time when she least expected it or deserved it but most needed it, Gert reported that a warm light began to move toward her enveloping her in a sense of love that she had never experienced before from anyone, especially from her father. She was given a sense that her life somehow mattered to the Source behind all reality and that there was a meaningful future for her in spite of her past. This healing embrace lasted for several minutes and, when the intensity began to subside, even though it was by then the middle of the night, she picked up her phone, called her business manager and said breathlessly, "Bring me a copy of the Holy Bible as quickly as you can!" Her manager knew her quite well and could not contain his shock. He blurted out, "My God, Gert, what has happened to you?" To which, she softly replied, "My God has happened to me."

I contend that this is the way the Ingenious Alchemist responds continually to folk as they move out of their circle of freedom. The loveliest truth I know is that God lives at the end of our ropes. The medieval mystics were fond of saying that our situations of extremities are often God's opportunities. Most of the people who have been through a twelve-step, self-help program report that when they get to the place where they have to admit that life is unmanageable and every decision brings nothing but greater grief, there appears a grace to help in such times of trouble. It does not come because people have deserved it or acted in ways that cause it to happen. The deepest characteristic of God's grace is that is completely unconditional. No wonder the hymn writer John Newton called it "amazing," for when we get to what seems like the end of our ropes, we discover that we are not at the end of gracious opportunities.

I believe that the essence of the Christian Gospel is embedded in this astonishing old story of Jacob. Like him, we did nothing to deserve birth, for it was and is total windfall, sheer gift. Our very existence grows out of the vision that God is ultimately pure generosity and One whose only intention is to bless. The deepest truth is that there is nothing we can do to make God love us more than God already loves us and nothing we can do to make God stop loving us. The One who is behind all things is nothing but love, always has been and always will be.

Jacob's response to his incredible dream encounter was utter astonishment. The only words he could muster were, "Surely God was in this place but I knew it not." I look on this statement as an accurate description of our religious condition. God is with us and for us always, but the problem is that we are not always aware of those wondrous Arms of Mercy underneath and all around us. Religious experience does not consist of something being created that did not exist before. Rather, it is suddenly awakening to the endless graciousness that has always been present but, until then, unperceived. Thomas Merton once described it as "the breakthrough to the Already."

A good friend of mine began his life with a profound sense of being a "nobody," devoid of any worth at all. He attempted to resolve these negative feelings by achieving academically, and he was quite successful. He eventually graduated with honors from both Harvard and Princeton, and even published a book that merited wide acclaim. However, he told me later that all these accomplishments reminded him of eating cotton candy, because there was a moment of intense sweet satisfaction only to be followed by the taste of emptiness once more.

Years later, he was asked to give a scholarly paper to an esteemed academic society. This was something he had dreamed of doing for a long time. However, at the conclusion of his presentation, that old "cotton candy experience" of disillusionment repeated itself again. He told me that he went back to his hotel room in midtown Manhattan, got down on his knees, and, even though he was a sophisticated and highly educated person, found himself crying out the famous words of the Bible's Philippian jailer, "What must I do to be saved?" He reported that, at that moment, a hand suddenly appeared on the wall before him, and the following words began to materialize: "Nothing, nothing at all. It comes with the territory. Your worth was bequeathed to you the moment you were conceived. From the foundations of the earth, God wanted you to be and God values you as you are."

In those words, "nothing, nothing at all," it finally dawned on my friend that his worth was not contingent upon his achieving. It was a gift from God as surely as his birth and every single breath had been. In that moment, he remembered an old image that he had encountered years before. It was that of a man riding on an ox, looking for an ox. Here was a person anxiously surveying the whole horizon when, all along, what he was seeking was right beneath him and always had been. This is exactly what happened to Jacob that night on the rocky hilltop, and I offer it to you as an insight into the mystery of the Holy One and an avenue for your own experience of hope.

Recall, if you will, the drawing of the two concentric circles in the Introduction: the inner circle of human freedom surrounded by the reality of Divine Ingenuity. No matter how one chooses to exercise one's freedom, even the most destructive actions enter the realm of the Ingenious Alchemist, and the great good news is that God is capable of doing something redemptive with absolutely everything! Consider all the bad choices that were made in the story of Jacob's early life. All of these characters were badly flawed and tragically destructive. Yet, even the worst misguided actions were not ultimate in their effects. God was able to take Isaac's religious indifference, Esau's superficial unawareness, Rebecca's cunning manipulation, and Jacob's arrogant exploitations and turn all of these destructive behaviors into occasions of growth and blessing. Centuries later, St. Paul was surely correct when he affirmed that "all things work together for good for those who love God" (Romans 8:28). As an old rabbi once said to me, "Despair is presumptuous. It is saying something about the future that we have no right to say. If God can make the things that *are* out of the things that *are not*, and can make dead things come to life again, who are we to set limits on what that kind of potency might yet do with what we have done?" I see this as the deepest of all truth and invite you to image the Holy as One who in the worst of times can do the best of things.

CHAPTER 2

Writing Straight
with Crooked Lines

The pages of Holy Scripture set side by side two great mysteries. St. Paul gives expression to this paradox in these famous words from his letter to the Philippians: "Work out your own salvation with fear and trembling; for it is God who is at work in you, enabling you both to will and to work for his good pleasure" (Philippians 2:12–13). What you have here are *both* the realities of what we humans do in the exercise of our God-given freedom *and* what God does from the depths of God's own being. The testimony of the Bible is that both of these energies are the source of the drama of history. Life, as we know it, is profoundly collaborative, although the precise delineation between what we do and what God does will always remain in the realm of mystery. The central contention of this book is that we must honor both of these participants and hold firmly to the hope that, while Divine ingenuity never abolishes human freedom, it does possess the potency to transform even the worst of actions into occasions for growth and blessing.

What I have been describing is very much in evidence as we pick up the story of Jacob where we left him on the rocky hilltop near the ancient city of Luz. Jacob is able to find his way successfully to his uncle in Haran, and the events that occur there reflect both a human being with genuine freedom and a God of amazing resourcefulness.

Upon arriving at Laban's abode in the land from which both Abraham and Rebecca had migrated, Jacob immediately falls in love with his beautiful first cousin, a gracious lady named Rachel. It is one of the earliest historical episodes of genuine romance. We need to remember that, in that era of the human saga, most marriage choices were arranged by older members of one's family. The age of romanticism came much later, but it was "love at first sight" for Jacob in relation to Rachel. When he told Rachel's father how he felt about her, Laban sized up the situation quite adroitly and proposed that Jacob work for him for seven years to earn the privilege of marrying her. It was a proposition to which Jacob happily agreed and, in one of the loveliest descriptions in all of Scripture about the true nature of romantic affection, those seven years "seemed to him but a few days" because of his great love for her (Genesis 29:20).

At the end of the seven years that Jacob worked and waited to marry Rachel, a wedding date was set, and the capacity of human beings to act destructively broke in rudely upon the scene. Rachel had an older sister named Leah who was Rachel's polar opposite in terms of feminine beauty. Leah was probably an Albino with highly unattractive weak eyes, and her father took the occasion to do an awesomely deceptive thing. Weddings in those days were lengthy affairs with lots of celebrating and drinking, so by the time of the actual wedding, Jacob was terribly drunk and his bride was appropriately veiled. On the morning after that first night, Jacob discovered to his horror that Laban had given him Leah rather than Rachel and, needless to say, he was furious. When confronted, Laban deftly informed him that the custom in that culture was that the elder sister had to be given in marriage before the younger could marry, so he had no choice. Quickly sensing the depth of Jacob's rage, Laban said, "You can go ahead and have Rachel as a wife now, but you will have to serve me for seven more years to fulfill your obligation."

Let me pause for a moment and simply note how the characteristics of deception can proliferate in an impaired family system. Laban's sister, Rebecca, had been willing to bend the rules of truth in a cause that she deemed worthy. Her brother demonstrated the same shape of character in this action of deception, which illustrates the truth of the modern cliché "what goes around comes around." The net result of all of this was that Jacob not only wound up with two wives in a time when bigamy was socially acceptable, but more importantly, he was indentured for seven more years of servitude to a clever opportunist of an uncle.

You can see in this story the great latitude that human beings possess in choosing how they come out of the circle of freedom. Destructiveness and injury befell several of the actors in this particular drama, and the level of agony only increased as the story unfolded. It turned out that Rachel, the beloved, proved to be barren after seven years of waiting, mysteriously unable to conceive and bear children, which in her time and culture was considered a serious female failing. On the other hand, Leah was extremely fertile and was able to produce four sons for Jacob, although there is no mention of any increase of affection towards her on Jacob's part for having done so. One of the tragic heroines in this heartless chain of events is the "ugly duckling," Leah. She openly made her fertile superiority to Rachel quite clear, and this, of course, increased her younger sister's frustration immeasurably.

In a last gasp of desperation, Rachel followed the example of Jacob's grandmother, Sarah, and gave Jacob her handmaiden, Bilhah, as a surrogate wife in her stead. Eventually, Bilhah was able to give Jacob two more sons, whom Rachel could claim as her own. Once again, you have an ancient social custom of accepted polygamy that differs drastically from today's "family values." As all this was unfolding, Leah ceased to be fertile and, in reaction to Rachel's ploy, supplied Jacob with yet another surrogate wife, a slave named Zilpah, who subsequently gave birth to the seventh and eighth sons of the prolific Jacob. Then, as mysteriously as Leah had experienced barrenness years before, she suddenly became fertile again and two more sons and a daughter were added to the growing list of Jacob's heirs. This meant that, over a period of a little more than a decade, Jacob now had ten sons by three different mothers and the extra bonus of a daughter as well.

Then, the totally unexpected occurred once again. Rachel, Jacob's beloved, was finally able to conceive and present to the patriarch, Jacob, the son for which she had fervently longed and made the object of unnumbered prayers. He was named Joseph, the eleventh son to be born to Jacob, but this child was given the special feelings that Jacob had for Rachel, and was regarded in a very real sense as the firstborn.

Needless to say, these interactions within a single-family system created all sorts of tension, and the situation was made worse by the working relationship between the uncle and the nephew. When the second seven-year obligation had run its course, Jacob negotiated with Laban to become entrepreneurial in his own right. Jacob proved to be even wilier and more manipulative than his conniving old uncle and, in time, this caused the space between them to become so acrimonious that Jacob quietly gathered up his extensive family and considerable wealth and fled from Haran before Laban realized what was happening.

The old man was able to catch up with him quickly but, by then, the breach between them was so vast that they parted ways, never to see each other again. Laban returned to Haran and Jacob made his way back to Canaan where his twin brother, Esau, whom he had deceived, was alive and well and very mindful of the events of the past. Not surprisingly, as glad as Jacob was to get away from Laban, the prospect of having to face his brother, Esau, was undeniably a frightening one.

Everything came to a dramatic climax one night by a little stream called Jabbock. Word had reached Jacob that Esau had learned of his homecoming and was moving toward him with a large group of armed men. Forever the cunning and wily one, Jacob sent all kinds of gifts ahead, along with his wives and children, in hope of softening Esau's hostility. Jacob remained behind, alone in the darkness just as he had been years before as a new exile.

At that moment, he had yet another fateful encounter with the Holy One. Jacob found himself being attacked by a mysterious figure who is never clearly identified. These two struggled fiercely all night long and the upshot of the whole incident was similar to what had happened decades before on the rocky hilltop near Luz. Once again, Jacob experienced the incredible truth that God's goodness is bigger than all human badness, and that God's power and willingness to forgive are greater than the human capacity to sin. Jacob discovered that the Holy One was more interested in his future than in his past, which is the foundation of God's being the Ingenious Alchemist.

What follows this awesome night of conflict is yet another confirmation of this image of the Holy. Beyond Jacob's wildest hopes, Esau was forgiving and compassionate. The Merciful One had obviously been at work "cleansing the thoughts" of Esau's heart, for what Jacob encountered from the one whom he had treated so shamelessly was exactly what he had sensed the night before—everlasting mercy and unconditional forgiveness. Behold, what Jacob had feared to be "the worst thing" possible turned out not to be "the last thing" in God's redemptive hands. Once again, grace had transmuted the "lead" of so much evil into the "gold" of authentic blessing.

However, life for Jacob did not remain all sweetness and light. Soon after these tumultuous events, Rachel died giving birth to a second son named Benjamin, and this enormous loss sent Jacob into a period of tremendous grief. One of the ways that Jacob responded to his sorrow was to transfer the intense affection he had always felt for Rachel to her first-born son, Joseph. This pattern of behavior set the stage for an incredible string of conflicts in what was obviously, to use a modern term, a "dysfunctional family." Jacob showed conspicuous favoritism to his eleventh son. He asked nothing of him in terms of work or responsibility and gave him special gifts, like the famous coat that the King James translation of the Bible describes as a garment of "many colors." A better understanding of the original language has revealed that a "coat with long sleeves" is a more accurate rendering of the term, and this only adds detail to the folly of Jacob's parenting style. A coat of this sort was highly unusual in that period of history. One could hardly do the vigorous work of caring for animals in such a piece of clothing. Only a prince or someone exempt from physical labor would wear such a garment, all of which underlines the tensions that were brewing right under the surface of this family.

The effects of Jacob's partiality were destructive to everyone involved. Not surprisingly, Joseph became an utterly arrogant and spoiled young child. He openly shared the dreams he had in his youth that reflected the grandiose self-image he had developed. He predicted that everyone else in the family would bow down to him because of his superiority. He was not above tattling on his older brothers to his father, creating even greater hostility between the two generations of father and sons. Naturally, the ten older brothers deeply resented Jacob's whole pattern of behavior to everyone: to their mothers who were unloved, to themselves for the unfair discrimination from their father, and to this pampered pet named Joseph who was becoming increasingly insufferable.

There is a deep irony in the path that Jacob chose to take as a father. It would seem that, of all people, Jacob should have known better, for he himself had suffered terribly years before when his father, Isaac, had openly loved Esau more than him. In that ancient culture, a mother's love did not have the powerful significance of a father's blessing, and much of Jacob's early formation was scarred by Isaac's unwise expenditure of paternal affection. The British historian H. G. Wells once wrote, "What we learn from history is that we do not learn from history." One of the amazing failures of our human species is our propensity to let the experiences of the past be wasted on us. Frederick Buechner has put "listening to your life" at the top of his hierarchy of human values, and this is precisely what Jacob did not do when it came to being a father. I once heard Dr. Martin Luther King Jr. preach a memorable sermon, using as his text Jesus' prayer from the cross, "Father, forgive them for they know not what they do." His main thesis was that much of the world's suffering results not from human badness, but from human blindness. It is the sin of unawareness and the refusal to learn from the events of the past that create so much of the anguish that plagues our world.

It does not take extraordinary imagination to see how Jacob's way of relating had explosive potential indeed. A father who loved unwisely, a son who was favored unfairly, and ten sons who were never loved appreciably were the ingredients of "a witch's brew" indeed. It all came to a head one fateful day far away from the tents of Jacob. The ten older brothers were no strangers to hard work and explicit responsibilities. They were shepherds like all their forebears before them, which meant they had to range widely over the open fields of Canaan to find water and suitable grazing pastures. With remarkable insensitivity, Jacob suggested one day that the seventeen-year-old Joseph go out into the fields and bring back word of how the industrious part of the family was doing. To amplify the obtuseness of both Jacob and Joseph, the lad attired himself in that hated "leisure coat" and ventured forth naively. When the ten unloved sons saw the image of this spoiled brat sauntering proudly over the horizon, years of pent-up rage at both Jacob and Joseph erupted violently. For the first time in their lives, they had access to Joseph away from their father, and it seemed at first that they would tear him limb from limb and kill him with their own bare hands. However, the oldest of Jacob's sons, Leah's firstborn named Reuben, came to his senses quickly and realized that fratricide was a grievous offense. He suggested that they put Joseph down in a dried up well and take time to think things out more rationally.

The brothers scattered to go about their work and Reuben secretly planned to retrieve Joseph all by himself and take him back to Jacob with the story of his heroic rescue. I can picture in my mind's eye the desperate hope of the real "firstborn son" to gain finally the love and acceptance of the one who had sired him but never esteemed him. This is yet another sign of just how fractured and polarized the whole family system had become.

However, Rueben's ploy never had the opportunity to materialize. The other brothers came back to the well before Rueben and, at that very moment, a caravan of Midianite traders happened by on their way to Egypt. A younger son of Leah named Judah exclaimed, "Why not sell Joseph as a slave to these travelers? That way he is out of our lives forever and we do not have to bear his blood on our hands." It proved to be a cunning alternative to their initial murderous instincts, so they stripped Joseph of that despised coat, settled on the price of twenty shekels of silver, and Joseph was taken off to be a slave in the most inhuman culture of all the ancient world.

To complete their malice, the brothers dipped "the coat with sleeves in it" in goat blood, took it back to Jacob, and said innocently, "We found this in the fields. Is this Joseph's coat?" Jacob concluded the obvious from the sight of this bloodstained garment, and went into a period of grief that was every bit as profound as when he had lost his beloved wife, Rachel. My conjecture is that the intensity of this reaction must have caught the half-brothers by surprise. They had been so wounded by the unhealthiness of Jacob's favoritism and all that it had done to disrupt the family that they did not realize the depth of affection that Jacob felt for the one they had come only to loath and despise.

Jacob's grief did not abate as weeks and months went by. It must have been agonizing for his ten surviving sons to hear their father say, "I shall go down to Sheol to my son, mourning," when, all the while, they knew that they had willfully caused this anguish (Genesis 37:35). Jacob's way of responding to his grief is a cautionary tale for all of us. It is profoundly true that an experience of great bereavement is always "a Gethsemane moment," in that as grievers, we do not get our way. This can be a very perilous moment spiritually. I have known many a person's trusting relationship to God to disintegrate in "the valley of the shadow of grief." It needs to be noted that Jacob's resolve never to be consoled was a choice that he intentionally made and was not an inevitable necessity.

I vividly remember a moment that occurred about two months after the death of my ten-year-old daughter in 1970. The three of us who remained of our immediate family unit went, for the first time after my daughter died, to a little restaurant where the four of us had often dined before. As we sat down, the sight of the empty chair there beside me sent a wave of incredible pain to the heart of my very being. It symbolized what had happened to our circle of love, and I remember thinking, "Stop the world. I want to get off. I simply cannot stand the pain of being in a world in which Laura Lue is no longer a part." However, as these thoughts coursed through my mind, my eyes shifted to my twelve-year-old son sitting across from me. He was as sad as the rest of us were and seemed so fragile and vulnerable at that moment. From somewhere the thought came, "Wait a minute. For all you have lost, there is still much remaining that is worthy of love. You have a family who needs you, a career, and a life that beckons to be fulfilled." That was the moment that I resolved to rejoin the human race and, although still filled with excruciating pain, I stooped over and began to pick up the pieces of a shattered life and set out to explore what could be made of what was left. This is not what Jacob decided to do in the midst of his grief, but notice that his response was a choice of his own making. Psychologist Victor Frankel called this "our final human freedom." It is not within our power to determine what happens to us circumstantially, but we can determine how we will respond to what life does to us.

One of the many ironies of the Jacob saga is the aphorism that we have noted before: "what goes around comes around." Here is a case of one who had shamelessly deceived his old, blind father having the same kind of deceit being done to him! The Scriptural connection between what we sow and what we reap is one facet of the reality in which we find ourselves, yet it is not the whole story because of the presence and action of the Ingenious

Alchemist. For example, seeing Jacob grieve as he did made a profound impression on the very ones who had perpetuated his suffering. The ten older sons' anger over their legitimate grievance was gradually transmuted into greater compassion for this flawed and all-too-human father. We will see in the next chapter what all of those events did in the life of Joseph. The whole point here is that we are called to stay open in hope in relation to The Great Not Yet. We must resist the temptation to rush too quickly to judgment regarding the nature of any event. The wiser approach is what the Bible calls "waiting upon the Lord." If we are still breathing, it is too early to tell about the ultimate impact of any event in our lives.

I once heard the late Dr. Carlyle Marney preach an unforgettable Easter sermon entitled "God's Strong Hands." He focused essentially on the part that Judas Iscariot played in the closing hours of Jesus' life. However, his conclusion came as a surprise to me. He said, "The final tragedy of Judas did not consist of what he did. It was undeniably shameful for him to betray his best friend, but not all that much worse than what the other eleven disciples did in abandoning Jesus completely. No," he continued, "his ultimate tragedy lay in what he did not do; he did not stay

around to see what God could do with human defection."
This is the sin of coming to closure prematurely, just as
suicide is usually a poor and permanent solution to a tem-
porary problem that might be resolved in time. I recalled
Marney's sermon when, years later, he told me of how he
was dramatically snapped out of a prolonged period of
depression toward the end of his life. He was an avid gar-
dener and, one afternoon in the midst of terrible emotional
heaviness, he was sitting listlessly among his plants when
the thought suddenly came to him, "Roses grow out of
horse manure!" He was startled as the realization dawned
on him that if the loveliest and most fragrant of blossoms
could emerge from the smelliest and most repulsive of
substances, who was he to set limits on what the Creator
of this mysterious world could yet do? This is as fine an
affirmation of God as the Ingenious Alchemist as I have
ever heard. When literally taken to heart, it can become a
reliable foundation of hope.

CHAPTER 3

The Gift of Resilience—
Never, Never Give Up!

Many years ago, a recovering alcoholic named Dennis Worley wrote a book entitled: *When the Worst That Can Happen Already Has.* It is a collection of stories about individuals who had made heroic responses to situations in their lives that were truly horrific. My sense is that the biblical character of Joseph could have easily contributed to such a volume for, as we saw at the end of the last chapter, his life suddenly took an unexpected turn that seemed, on the surface, to be utterly devastating.

The first seventeen years of his life had been a time of exceptional privilege. He was the twelfth child born into the family of a powerful patriarch, but he was the first offspring whom his mother had been able to bear and, since she was "the love of his father's life," when she died giving birth to a second child, his grieving father transferred all of his special affection to Joseph in a most unwise fashion. In our kind of world, injustice always breeds chaos. The yen for fairness runs deep and wide in our particular species. This travesty of parenting ended violently with Joseph being sold into slavery to some traders headed for Egypt, and the aged father, Jacob, being deceptively misled about Joseph's final fate.

One can only imagine the inner turmoil that Joseph must have experienced when the bottom dropped out of his life as he had known it. He was an overly protected "hot-house plant" if there ever was one. He never had to work a day in his life and, undoubtedly, had been systematically shielded from almost all the discomforts to which most humans are exposed. It is a miracle of sorts that Joseph was able to survive this radical change of fortune at all, but a single phrase that occurs in these stories, again and again, suggests the secret of his survival: "the Lord was with him." What was true for Joseph is also true for us: God never abandoned Joseph and will never abandon us either. We often forget the Holy One, but the Holy One never forgets us.

Joseph's fortunes took a dramatic upturn when the Midianite traders sold him to a highly placed Egyptian official named Potiphar, Chief of the Pharoah's security guards. What happened next was truly surprising. For the first time in his life, something was expected of Joseph. He was put to work and given responsibilities within the structure of a well-run household and, as a result, this seventeen-year-old began to flower. Joseph had obviously inherited many natural gifts from both of his highly capable parents, but because nothing had ever been asked of him, those creative capacities were never recognized or developed. The amazing truth was that Joseph began to flourish developmentally in ways that he might never have done had he remained pampered by his indulgent father. Here is yet another example of how the Ingenious Alchemist turned what seemed to be truly tragic into an occasion of genuine growth. I once saw a grave stone in a country cemetery that bore the following inscription: "In the worst of times, he did the best of things." These words accurately describe the way Joseph responded to what seemed to be a daunting turn of events in his life.

Potiphar was by no means blind to the treasure that he had acquired in this gifted young Hebrew slave. Month by month, Joseph was given increasing responsibilities and, because he discharged these duties so effectively, it was not too long before he became the chief steward of Potiphar's whole household. Although it was a relatively small human system, it still represented a remarkable accomplishment on the part of someone who had never before been asked to produce creatively.

In the midst of real success, however, a shadow began to fall again across Joseph's fortunes. Potiphar's wife began to develop a host of inappropriate feelings for the handsome young slave, and, before too long, she started trying to seduce him in unavoidably direct ways. The origin of these impulses will always remain a mystery, but it may have had something to do with Potiphar's probable castration, done in order to qualify for his position in the royal palace. The Pharaohs were so protective of their sizeable harems that only males who were rendered eunuchs were considered safe enough to intermingle with all of these women. This would have put unnatural stress on the wives of these men in Pharaoh's inner circle, and it could be that Lady Potiphar was acting out of genuine deprivation when she made these seductive overtures to Joseph.

Joseph's response to Lady Potiphar reflects the fact that he had matured remarkably. He pointed out that he had been given extensive authority over Potiphar's business and household affairs, but that did not include the unique bond between his master and his master's wife.

The way that Joseph reacted reminds me of an experience that a trusted friend and minister once reported to me. It seems that a couple in the parish he was serving became close personal friends to him and his wife. They often socialized together and even traveled to distant places in each other's company. My friend told me that this particular man died quite unexpectedly of a heart attack in his early forties and, because of their close friendship, my friend was particularly sensitive in the kind of pastoral care that he extended to this widow. About a year after her husband's death, this woman acknowledged to the minister that she had come to feel much more for him than that of a church member for her pastor. "I have fallen in love with you," she confessed and waited for his response. He carefully replied by commending her for her honesty and thanked her for the compliment embedded in those words. But then he said: "I need to make clear that, given the commitment that I have already made to my wife, I am not eligible for the

49

kind of relationship that you are suggesting. I can be your pastor and your friend, but I will not be your lover."

Here was someone who clearly understood the meaning and importance of boundaries when it comes to healthy human relationships, and this is how Joseph chose to respond to Lady Potiphar's advances that day. Unfortunately, she was not easily thwarted. She continued to press her case and, one day when the two of them were alone, she grabbed hold of Joseph physically in an effort to have him engage with her sexually. In response to her advance, Joseph broke out of her embrace and fled from the room. In all this commotion, she managed to keep hold of his outer garment. This rejection proved to be the last straw for her. The old adage "Hell hath no fury like a woman scorned" certainly applies to this situation, for Potiphar's wife was so incensed by Joseph's behavior that she proceeded to turn the tables on the young slave and told her husband that Joseph had done to her what she, in fact, had done to him. She even produced the outer garment as evidence of an unwanted attack.

Such an accusation was as explosive in that culture as any sexual overture of a black male toward a white female was regarded in the South where I grew up. My sense is that Potiphar did not believe the veracity of his wife's charge because, if he had, Joseph would have been executed on the spot. But Potiphar removed Joseph immediately from the household to maintain peace with his wife and placed him in the imperial prison, which was under Potiphar's command.

How shattering this demotion must have seemed to the young Hebrew. Once again, as with his brothers long before, the bottom suddenly fell out of a life that had been truly satisfying to him and, this time, the issue of blatant injustice made the pill even harder to swallow. Looking back, Joseph could see how his arrogant and grandiose behavior had, in part, precipitated his own brothers' outrage, but, in this situation, he had heroically done the honorable thing and look where it got him! If ever there were justification to throw up one's hands and say, "I quit," this would have been such a moment.

However, once again, the account in Genesis affirms that "the Lord was with him," and evidence of that can be seen in the character of Joseph's response. He did not dissolve into despair and cry out, "Why me? Why this injustice?" but rather stooped over patiently to pick up the broken fragments of his life and ask simply, "What can I do now? How can I not just make the best of things, but make the most of these circumstances?"

The practical difference between asking, "What can I do now?" instead of protesting, "Why me?" is enormous indeed. Joseph proceeds to do the very best thing he could do in that terribly difficult situation: he became a servant to the needs of the other prisoners around him.

In the middle of the 1930s, an American named Langdon Gilkey went to interior China to teach at a private academy there. He had just graduated from Harvard University and honestly believed that education was the answer to all of life's problems. He was thoroughly convinced that if you taught a person the difference between right and wrong, he or she would do what was right.

When World War II broke out and Japan captured mainline China, all the Allied citizens in that country were rounded up and sent to a camp called Shantung Compound, in which prisoners of war were incarcerated. Fifteen hundred British, American, Canadian, and Dutch folk were crowded into a space that had been built to house no more than three hundred. While they were not abused or killed as the Germans had done to the Jews, the living conditions were very cramped and the food rations were painfully scant indeed.

Gilkey was amazed at how these conditions of deprivation affected the prisoners. Most of them were missionaries and educators who had come to China with the most humane and altruistic of motivations. However, when their own welfare and the provision for their families were threatened, fear literally dehumanized these formerly idealistic professionals, and they became ruthless competitors with each other, stealing food and stooping to outrageously destructive interactions among themselves.

Any sense of the common good quickly evaporated among the prisoners in that trying situation, except for one small group—some Dutch Roman Catholic monks who remembered the words of their Lord: "The one who would be greatest among you must be a servant of all." These simple monastics were willing to do for all others whatever needed to be done, be it working in the kitchen, mopping the floor, or listening to fellow prisoners who were overwhelmed with fear. They opened Langdon Gilkey's eyes about what was truly foundational in life: not just an intellectual grasp of what was right, but a trust in the sufficiency of God's universe that enables one to serve in love, regardless of the circumstances.

Joseph chose to live his life in the dreary confines of the royal prison with a trusting and serving heart, just as the Roman Catholic monks had done in Shantung Compound. He found himself at the absolute bottom of the social hierarchy—a foreign-born slave and a prisoner—but that did not keep him from paying attention to others and doing whatever he could to meet their needs. Once again, who can fail to see the permeating influence of the Ingenious Alchemist?

The emergence of a "serving heart" is evidence that Joseph had experienced real personal growth since his turbulent childhood and adolescence in Canaan. We need to remember how astonishingly insensitive to other people he had been in days gone by, when he was openly sharing his grandiose dreams and going blithely to see his working brothers while he had no responsibilities whatsoever. In today's psychological jargon his outlook might have been described as "malignant narcissism." Joseph was the epitome of indifference and unawareness of others while under the influence of his doting father, but the trauma of his brothers' actions and his life in Potiphar's household awakened a whole new range of mature sensitivities within him. Now the outside world of people was not only noticed by Joseph but also valued and taken seriously. What happened to others now mattered to him, and this capacity of empathy played a crucial role in the unfolding of his personal destiny.

Joseph was incarcerated in the Imperial Prison where enemies of the state were carefully placed. Two of his fellow inmates turned out to be part of the most intimate circle of the Pharoah's servants: namely, his personal butler and the chief baker. The government of Egypt at that time was a ruthless autocracy. The Pharaoh ruled without any checks or balances upon his authority, and so the famous words of the English statesman Lord Acton apply here: "Power tends to corrupt and absolute power tends to corrupt absolutely." The Pharaohs were famous for acting violently on the slightest whim or feeling and both the butler and the baker must have offended the Pharaoh in ways that led to their being imprisoned like Joseph.

Both of them were utterly shaken by this trauma, and one of the ways that their anxiety expressed itself was through terrible nightmares. Joseph was quick to notice how strained they appeared every morning, and they responded to his concern by sharing the images that haunted them in the night.

One of the more notable gifts that Joseph possessed was the ability to make sense of these nocturnal events, and, out of the purest and most positive intentions, he told them what he thought the dreams meant. Amazingly, it came to pass that his insights proved to be true. For example, he surmised that the baker was probably in more serious trouble than he had realized and might have been implicated in a plot to poison the Pharaoh. Sure enough, within a matter of hours, the baker was taken out and executed. At the same time, the butler was exonerated from the charge against him and given back his cherished position of waiting personally on the ruler, just as Joseph had told him would happen after hearing the butler's dream. As the butler was joyously taking leave of the prison, Joseph said plaintively, "Please remember me when you get out. I am incarcerated although I have committed no criminal offense and I ask that you consider returning the favor of helping me as I have helped you." I regard this as yet another sign of Joseph's growing maturity in that he was not too proud to ask for help. Let's face it, there is no such thing as a self-made human being. In large part, we are each what we are because of our interactions with others, and Joseph was humble enough to recognize that salient fact and to act upon it.

Unfortunately, the sad truth was that the elated butler forgot all about the caring friendship of his fellow prisoner. Two long years went by as Joseph tediously languished in that dead-end imprisonment. Among our worst human traits are the tendencies to forget or to take for granted "the goodness and mercy that have followed us all the days of our lives" (Psalm 23), such as what others have done to help us. How wearing those long months must have been for Joseph, and what a temptation it must have been to give up in hopeless despair. Nevertheless, the continuing marvel in all of this was the amazing patience and perseverance of Joseph's trust in the God of his forebears.

I once heard the reality of faith described as "living above S-E-E-level," that is, not allowing the surface appearance of what we see to be the only factor in how we perceive reality. I had a spiritual mentor say to me years ago, "God never asks us to feel a certain way, but rather to trust him no matter how we feel!" Such a stance is difficult to maintain indeed, but with the help of the Ingenious Alchemist, Joseph was managing to do just that when another series of dramatic events sent the saga of his life in an altogether new direction.

This time it was the Pharaoh himself who had recurring disturbing dreams. The Egyptians were notoriously sensitive to these forms of human experience. They believed their gods worked the night shift. They considered dreams to be one of the ways that impending doom was often foreshadowed. When the Pharaoh dreamed night after night that seven fat cows were suddenly devoured by seven gaunt and emaciated creatures, he awoke in anxious distress. A whole "cottage industry" of dream interpreters existed at that time, but none of these individuals could decipher these images to the Pharaoh's satisfaction. This problem soon became the concern of the entire palace staff, which prompted the reinstated butler to remember the young Hebrew slave who had been so helpful to him years before. It was a sign of the Pharaoh's desperation that such an unlikely resource was allowed to be useful.

With his amazing interpretive gifts, Joseph went straight to the heart of the meaning of the Pharaoh's dream and suggested, "We are on the threshold of seven years of unbelievable agricultural abundance, which the seven fat cows symbolize. However, this will be followed by seven years of famine." Joseph proposed that the wisest response to such a possibility would be to set aside a portion during all the years of surplus and store that for the subsequent season of scarcity. Such a strategy would be a way of staving off the threat of starvation in the future. The Pharaoh was amazed. It was the first time that anyone's interpretation of his dream had made sense. In a manner consistent with the absolute power that was a Pharoah's to wield, in one royal fiat he elevated Joseph from his status as an imprisoned slave to the number two position of power in all of Egypt, giving him the authority to confiscate a percentage of the next seven years' worth of agricultural abundance and to store this in royal bins for any future emergency.

It was a stroke of political genius all the way around. Not only was it wise to save the current affluence for the proverbial rainy day, but it was also a deft move to let a non-Egyptian do the dirty work of collecting what was history's first windfall tax. Centuries later, the Romans were shrewd enough to do the same thing. They avoided becoming tax collectors themselves by letting certain local citizens absorb the hostility that such governmental assessments always incur. Joseph's elevation was an unbelievable turn of events for the whole country, as well as for Joseph himself. The insightful young Hebrew set about immediately executing this remarkably wise public policy that turned out to be enormously successful. History unfolded exactly as Joseph had foreseen and, when a region-wide period of famine ravaged the whole Mediterranean Basin, the descendants of Abraham were saved from extinction by the action of their very own brother whom they had callously exiled decades before.

This story raises the seminal issue of how we are to understand the relationship of the Holy One to the realities of time and history. Most opinions about this point have leaned toward two extremes. Many profound thinkers, such as Plato and John Calvin, contend that God is outside of the sequence of history and looks down upon the whole process from the distant vantage point of eternity. This means that God knows the future as clearly as the past and the present, and this is the basis of the celebrated doctrine of foreknowledge and predestination. It is easy to see how this story of Pharaoh's dreams and Joseph's predictions would support such a theological worldview.

In contrast, those at the other extreme contend that, as I have said earlier, God's purpose in creation was to make an experience of God's kind of joy available to creatures made in God's image. For that to be possible, such creatures had to be given a measure of freedom and the capacity to participate authentically in the shaping of history. Again and again in Holy Scripture, the reality of human freedom seems to be implied in statements such as: "Choose you this day whom you shall serve," or Jesus' lament, "Jerusalem! Jerusalem! How I would have gathered you like a hen gathers her chicks, but you would not." There is a passage in Genesis 22 in which God commands Abraham to take Isaac up on Mount Moriah and sacrifice him as a burnt offering. When Abraham amazingly obeys, God is reported to have said, "Now that I see you did not withhold your only son from me, the sacrifice need not be made, but a ram instead will suffice."

The implication in this story is that for history to have personal meaning for human beings, God intentionally chose not only to limit God's power so as to make room for human freedom, but also to limit God's knowledge of the future. This was not something imposed on God from outside, but was an internal choice so that the goal of experiencing God's joy could be realized. This implies that God is in the adventure of history with us, and the future is open to both God and to us to be mutually shaped. While God surely possesses the power to know the end from the beginning, God chooses not to exercise that power so that our participation in history can have meaning, instead of our being programmed like robots.

How could this theological vision fit with the saga of Pharaoh and Joseph? One could say that, while God does not already know the exact shape of The Great-Not-Yet, God does see quite deeply into the present and can sense the direction in which current decisions are moving. Joseph's interpretations could have grown out of what he presently saw in the abundance that was already flowering all around Egypt, and through his knowledge that it is not unusual for such ebb and flow cycles to occur in nature. God did not need to predestine the years of lean or plenty for a sensitive person to perceive them as Joseph did. These two ways of understanding time and eternity have long existed side by side and each person will have to decide which one seems the truest. My point in raising this issue is to suggest that predestination is not the only possibility resident in the events that happened to Joseph.

What does seem clear to me is that the image of God as the Ingenious Alchemist seems to radiate throughout all of these passages. Consider that if Jacob had not showed the favoritism that he did, neither Joseph nor his brothers would have matured as they did eventually. If the brothers had not sold Joseph into slavery in Egypt, he would have never been in a position to save so many from starvation, including his very own brothers who had caused him so much suffering. If Joseph had remained with Jacob, who never asked anything of him, he might not have matured as he did under Potiphar. Had Potipahr's wife not done what she did, Joseph would never have come to the attention of the Pharaoh. Time and time again, the human beings in this story come out of the circle of freedom in destructive ways, yet we see what the ingenious potency of the Holy One was able to do to transmute that "lead of evil" into the "gold of growth and blessing." What could be a more appropriate image than that of a resourceful and gracious Alchemist?

CHAPTER 4

Leopards Cannot Change Their Spots, But Humans Can

Once there was a young Scottish minister who, immediately after completing his training in seminary, was sent to serve a church in a little village up in the Scottish Highlands. Not long after his arrival, a young tenant farmer in his congregation was caught red-handed in the act of stealing. In that community, punishment was harsh and swift. In a matter of days, the thief was convicted and dispatched to a nearby penitentiary. The landowner for whom the tenant farmer worked was terribly distressed by his action, but had the firm belief that there was better potential in him than was indicated by what he had done on that fateful night. Therefore, the landowner allowed the thief's family to remain in their house and work for him. Periodically he would visit the prison to encourage the young man to learn from his mistakes.

When the tenant farmer had served his sentence, his former employer was so convinced of the young man's moral progress that he gave him back his old job and invited him to rejoin his family and the community. Not surprisingly, the majority of the landowner's neighbors were outraged by this action. They protested, "A leopard cannot change his spots. Once a thief, always a thief! We'll never sleep securely again knowing that culprit is back in our midst." They even initiated a formal campaign to petition the landowner to rescind his decision.

All of this was very grievous to the young minister, for there was only one "Kirk," as the church was called in that village, which meant that all the participants in this conflict came together every Sunday to worship side by side. One day, it dawned on the clergyman that he was seeing acted out before his very eyes exactly what Jesus had predicted when he gave the keys of the Kingdom to Simon Peter and the disciples, saying, "What you bind on earth will be bound in heaven, and what you loose on earth will be loosed in heaven." In the most concrete of terms, what the protesters were doing was "binding" the young tenant to his past actions. They were refusing to believe that significant change is possible for an adult human being, while the actions of the landowner were an attempt to "loosen" this one from his past and open him to the possibility of a genuinely different future.

This is a profoundly seminal issue for every time and place, and it is the basic dynamic at work as we approach the last segment of the Jacob saga and his interaction with all of his sons. It had been twenty-seven years since the family system had imploded and Joseph had been sold to become a slave in Egypt. We have followed the unexpected turns that his life had taken. In ways that no one could have anticipated, Joseph's career was even more legendary than Abraham Lincoln's famous journey from a log house to the White House. Through the exercise of his considerable range of gifts, Joseph enabled Egypt to become the bread-basket of the ancient world in a period of region-wide famine. When the effects of this trauma reached all the way east to Canaan, wily old Jacob decided to send his sons to Egypt to stave off the specter of wholesale starvation. It is important to note that he commissioned for this endeavor only the ten sons who had come into the world through the three unloved mothers. Beloved Rachel had given birth to two sons before her premature death, and Benjamin, as her last baby had become the object of special paternal affection. Jacob seemed to have learned some lessons from the pain of the past and he had not been as blatant in his show of favoritism to Benjamin as he had to Joseph; but there was still a distinct difference in the way he parceled out his love, as was demonstrated by the fact that Benjamin was kept safely at home while the others ventured southwest to Egypt.

When the ten sons of Jacob arrived in that ancient kingdom, the stage was set for an extraordinary set of interactions. Joseph had anticipated that the famine crisis might precipitate the reuniting of old adversaries. On the other hand, the brothers had no inkling that their despised sibling still lived.

What follows reminds one of the old television show *Candid Camera,* in which the audience knows things of which the characters in the drama are totally unaware. Joseph immediately recognized his brothers and accused them of being spies. They hastily denied the charges and began to explain who they were and where they had come from, which was exactly what Joseph was anxious to know because the welfare of his father and his only full brother was his primary concern. Eventually, he agreed to sell the ten sons some food, but claimed to doubt the truthfulness of their stories. He resolved to keep one of the brothers as a hostage until the rest returned with their youngest brother, Benjamin, to verify their account.

This strategy may appear to be revenge at the ones who had mistreated him so badly decades before but, more importantly, it was an inventive means to achieve his purpose. Joseph wanted to discover if the ten had grown at all through the events of the past. Did they feel toward Benjamin as they had felt toward him? Were they still as hostile to their father as had once been the case? Joseph himself had undergone tremendous changes in his whole personhood. Had anything comparable to this growth been taking place with the rest of his family in Canaan? He hoped that he would learn the answers to these questions from the test he had devised.

When the nine returned to Jacob without their brother and told him all that had transpired in Egypt, he was profoundly upset and angry that they had disclosed so much information about the family. He wanted to know, "Why did you have to go into the existence of Benjamin and let this foreigner in on what is solely our family business?" They replied that they had no choice in that situation but to be completely honest and were as perplexed as Jacob was by the whole disturbing scenario. The old patriarch staunchly refused even to consider the idea of allowing Benjamin to be taken to Egypt and the fate of the son being held hostage in that foreign land did not seem to be a matter of grave concern to him. Yet, in time, as the food secured in Egypt began to run out, Jacob changed his mind. Once again, the shrewd old Hebrew concluded that some odds were better than none at all and, thus, with utmost reluctance and sadness, he agreed to send the last heir of Rachel's on a fateful adventure indeed.

When the ten arrived in Egypt, Joseph was beside himself with joy. After almost three decades, he was reunited once again with his only full brother, and he brought in the hostage brother and entertained the entire entourage with a lavish Egyptian dinner. The next day, laden with food, the eleven sons of Jacob were sent on their way, and Joseph subtly set up one last ploy to discover if "the leopards had truly changed their spots."

Unbeknown to any of the brothers, Joseph had his royal drinking cup secretly slipped into Benjamin's bags of grain and, soon after they had set out for Canaan, he had his soldiers overtake them and accuse them of the crime of theft. Of course, the brothers staunchly denied these charges, but when Joseph's men conducted a search of their belongings, they found the cup in Benjamin's sack. They immediately arrested him and prepared to return him to Egypt. In shock, all of the brothers returned with Benjamin and, finally, Joseph discovered what he most wanted to know. To the man, all ten of the less loved sons pled with Joseph not to detain their youngest sibling. Simeon, the same brother who, decades before, had masterminded the selling of Joseph to the Midianite traders offered to take Benjamin's place and serve the life sentence instead of him. In one accord, the sons claimed that their aged father could not survive the loss of Rachel's other son, which made it clear to Joseph that his brothers had experienced authentic personal growth. They no longer bore the anger toward their father that they once felt because of his favoritism, nor did they harbor the resentment toward Benjamin that they once experienced in relation to Joseph.

Such a genuine maturing moved Joseph to the core. With an overwhelming flood of emotion, he revealed his true identity to them in the famous words: "I am your brother, Joseph!" There is no way to describe accurately the shock experienced by his brothers, but this was quickly followed by a time of festive celebration. The wounds of the past were swallowed up and transformed by the realities of grace and mercy. To their astonishment, Joseph bore no lasting grudges toward those who had once treated him so shamelessly. He instructed them to return to their father and tell him of this extraordinary turn of events and then bring him and the whole family back to Egypt to stay during the prolonged famine.

Obviously, discharging this challenge was extremely bittersweet for the ten brothers, for it required coming clean with Jacob about how they had mistreated both their own brother and callously deceived him, causing decades of unnecessary grief. Honest confession is often described as being good for the soul, but it also exacts a toll on the confessor's pride. Nonetheless, they revealed the whole sordid story to Jacob, and while the shock of it all was so great that he temporarily fainted, he was revived and was able to make the journey to Egypt to experience a joyous reconnection with the son that he had loved so much and had lost for so long. The whole clan successfully relocated in a new homeland and relished the restoration of affection that comes when past sins are forgiven and a new way of relating to each other begins to emerge.

Jacob was thus able to end his turbulent life in greater peace than he had ever known before, but the moment of his death created a new crisis for the ten brothers who had acted so harshly years before. The emotion of guilt is deep-rooted and very powerful indeed and, although the actions of Joseph had been unfailingly merciful, it was difficult for them to trust him totally. They feared that once their aged patriarch was dead, Joseph would wreak vengeance on them; and so, reminiscent of their earlier days, they manipulatively fabricated a story and told Joseph that their father's last words to them was to insist that Joseph was not to destroy them. Their fearfulness broke Joseph's heart, evoked a flood of tears, and moved him to say some of the most memorable words in all of Holy Scripture: "Do not be afraid! Am I in the place of God? Even though you intended to do harm to me, God intended it for good, in order to preserve a numerous people, as he is doing today. So have no fear; I myself will provide for you and your little ones" (Genesis 50:19–21).

These words are not only the climax of the Jacob saga, but are also the purest expression of the central contention of this book: namely, the image of the Holy One as an Ingenious Alchemist. It opens the way for us to believe that what God's resourceful goodness can do to evil, in terms of redemption, is finally greater than what evil can do to goodness, in terms of destructiveness. God's goodness is bigger than all the badness in this complicated world and this, of course, is the source of a hopefulness that can sustain one no matter what the circumstances.

Madeleine L'Engle has written a lovely little novel entitled *A Live Coal in the Sea.* The title comes from the following saying of a fifteenth-century mystic named William Langland: "But all the wickedness in the world which we may do or think is no more to the mercy of God than a live coal dropped in the sea." When you consider the vastness of the ocean and what it can do in relation to a tiny lump of burning coal, you get a sense of the true proportion between the realities of good and evil and a greater understanding of how St. Paul could claim: "But where sin increased, grace abounded all the more" (Romans 5:20). There is finally only one God in all the universe: nothing else is as big. Such an affirmation enables us to live in the present and move toward the future in genuine confidence. At the heart of that Mystery who stands behind all things is a loving and an Ingenious Alchemist.

Therefore, be not afraid or "afeared," as the ancients were fond of saying. Who knows what that kind of potency may yet do with whatever it is that you face in your own life?

Brave journey, dear hearts!

About the Author

John R. Claypool grew up in Nashville, Tennessee, and was educated at four different institutions of learning—Mars Hill College, Mars Hill, North Carolina; Baylor University, Waco, Texas; Southern Baptist Theological Seminary of the Southwest, Louisville, Kentucky; and The Episcopal Theological Seminary of the Southwest, Austin, Texas. He was ordained in 1953 as a Southern Baptist clergyman and served as senior pastor of congregations in Kentucky, Texas, and Mississippi for thirty-one years. In 1985, he moved to "another room of God's Great Church," and was ordained both as a deacon and a priest in the Episcopal Church in 1986. He served as associate rector of Christ Episcopal Church in San Antonio,

Texas, following his ordination, and in June of 1987, became the rector of Saint Luke's Episcopal Church in Birmingham, Alabama, a position he held until his retirement from full-time parish ministry in 2001. For the last four years he has been the professor of homiletics at Mercer University's McAfee School of Theology in Atlanta, Georgia. He and his wife Ann have three grown children and two grandchildren. They now make their home in Atlanta, where he is also a priest associate of All Saints Episcopal Church in the heart of that great city. He holds six honorary degrees along with his earned doctorate, and has written eleven books, including this volume.